# 627 Challenging Science & Nature Trivia Questions

Seven Phoenix, Ph.D., Editor

# DEDICATION

This book is dedicated to all the science trivia junkies out there.

# Table of Contents

# PREFACE

This volume of trivia came about for people who are seeking no-nonsense trivia questions for their own pub trivia night, personal entertainment, or to play with family and friends. These questions are essentially a "B-Side" to my main volumes of trivia, *American Pub Trivia*, of which two highly engaging and entertaining volumes have been published.

# 627 Challenging Science & Nature Trivia Questions

## Questions 1-10

1. It's the plasma atmosphere of the Sun that extends millions of miles into space, and most easily seen during a total solar eclipse. Or, a Mexican beer.

2. In physics, what do we call stored power due to position in an energy field?

3. Weaning a breast-feeding child is technically known as what?

4. Sukhoi is a major aircraft manufacturing company well known for its fighter planes until September of 2007, when it entered the commercial market. What country is Sukhoi in?

5. What's the scientific name for the breastbone? Special care should be taken when performing CPR not to break it.

6. Those who study pterodactyls, placoderms, stegosauruses & trilobites are in what field of science?

7. Embraer has seen dramatic growth in the 2000s due to demand for its E-Jets: narrow-body, twin-engine, medium-range, jet airliners. Where is Embraer headquartered?

8. What is classified as the consumption of 5 or more drinks in a row on at least one occasion?

9. In 1891, what inventor of the light bulb filed the first patent in the U.S. for a motion picture camera?

10. In what form of atomic decay, the least penetrative form of atomic decay, is the radioactive nucleus divided into a smaller nucleus and a particle consisting of two protons and two neutrons?

# Answers 1-10

1. Corona

2. Potential Energy

3. Ablactation

4. Russia

5. Sternum

6. Paleontology

7. Brazil

8. Binge Drinking

9. Thomas Edison

10. Alpha Decay

# Questions 11-20

11. Another of Ptolemy's original constellations, which constellation represents the ancient King of Aethopia in Greek mythology?

12. What measurement of pressure is defined as the pressure exerted by one Newton acting on an area of one square meter?

13. What atom is diamond, buckyball and graphite allotropes of?

14. What metallic, lustrous mineral earned the nickname "fool's gold?"

15. What was NASA's Space Transportation System more commonly known as?

16. How is medication to be taken if a prescription reads that is to be taken p.o.?

17. What trans-Neptunian dwarf planet is named for the creator of humanity in the Rapa Nui mythology of Easter Island since it was discovered around Easter of 2005?

18. What's do you call a plant that produces only leafy growth in its first year, and the flowering and dying in its second year?

19. Latin for "cross," this smallest constellation contains the stars more commonly referred to as The Southern Cross.

20. The disfiguring infectious condition, Hansen's disease, is also known as what?

# Answers 11-20

11. Cepheus

12. Pascal

13. Carbon

14. Pyrite

15. Space Shuttle

16. By Mouth

17. Makemake

18. Biennial

19. Crux

20. Leprosy

# Questions 21-30

21. Greek for "serpent-bearer," which constellation is considered by some to be the thirteenth Zodiac symbol?

22. What shape, from the Latin for "egg," is a figure constructed from two pairs of arcs, with two different radii, joined with smooth lines?

23. The pure form of this substance is a viscous clear liquid, like oil, and explains its old nickname "oil of vitriol."

24. Spastic colon is now diagnosed under the larger umbrella of what disorder?

25. These waves were accidentally discovered after a researcher walked by a radar tube and a chocolate bar melted in his pocket. Ironically, we now put Hot Pockets in them.

26. What do Senegal Chimpanzees use to sharpen their sticks into spears?

27. What are liquid rocks above ground called?

28. In the second law of thermodynamics, what tends to increase over time?

29. What process causes a tadpole to grow long legs, webbed feet and lose its tail? It's also a famous short story by Franz Kafka.

30. What is the observation of objects that reside in space more commonly known as?

## Answers 21-30

21. Ophiuchus

22. Oval

23. Sulfuric Acid

24. Irritable Bowel Syndrome

25. Microwaves

26. Teeth

27. Lava

28. Entropy

29. Metamorphosis

30. Astronomy

# Questions 31-40

31. What shape is a 5-pointed star drawn with 5 straight lines of equal length?

32. What type of igneous rock are the stones used in curling commonly made from?

33. Which Roman god of the sea shares his name with the planet furthest from the sun (not counting the dwarf planets)?

34. Which star-crossed love of Romeo lends her name to a moon of Uranus?

35. The theory of multiple intelligences, proposed by Howard Gardner in 1983, analyzes and better describes the concept of intelligence & addresses the question of whether what kind of tests are truly scientific?

36. What reputable scientific journal was first published on November 4, 1869?

37. What is the largest moon to orbit the planet Saturn?

38. Which bird is native to most of North America and is one of the few woodpecker species that migrate? It's also known as the Yellowhammer, clape, gaffer or harry-wicket?

39. What reusable knife blade is used for shaving hair?

40. The 15 chemical elements that are between actinium (89) and lawrencium (103) are called what?

# Answers 31-40

31. Pentagram

32. Granite

33. Neptune

34. Juliet

35. IQ Tests

36. Nature

37. Titan

38. Northern Flicker

39. Straight Razor

40. Actinides

# Questions 41-50

41. What is the measurement of the resistance of a fluid; its "thickness" or "internal friction?"

42. What marine mammal measures about the same length as a Boeing 737?

43. Which U.S. president formed the Space Task Group to study shuttle information and determine the feasibility of the shuttle program?

44. What abbreviated name was given to the 2000 Chimpanzee Health Improvement Maintenance & Protection Act, that was used to guarantee the welfare of research chimps?

45. What scientist was the first to observe bacteria in 1676?

46. Ancient Romans used what heavy metal to make their plumbing pipes, as well as in their cosmetics, long before it was discovered this metal is highly poisonous?

47. The overabundance of medical research for what disease led to a Federal moratorium on breeding chimps for research in 1996?

48. It's not just for breasts anymore! This polymer is more frequently being used to create bakeware, including cupcake molds, because of its non-toxicity and non-stick flexible surface.

49. What's the spanish-derived term for the nutrient rich excrement of bats?

50. This Larger Bear constellation is also known as The Big Dipper.

# Answers 41-50

41. Viscosity

42. Blue Whale

43. Nixon

44. CHIMP

45. Antony van Leeuwenhoek

46. Lead

47. HIV

48. Silicone

49. Guano

50. Ursa Major

# Questions 51-60

51. What is the theoretical temperature at which entropy would reach its minimum value, a condition in Kelvin degrees where a system does not emit or absorb energy (all atoms are at rest)?

52. What injury involves a temporary displacement of the end of a bone from a joint?

53. Encephalitis is an acute inflammation of what part of the body?

54. Until around 1600 A.D., it was commonly believed that this star attracted magnetized needles.

55. What is the number one doomsday scenario, according to "Discover Magazine"☐ in 2000?

56. What name is used when dolphins rush small fish into shallow waters for feeding purposes?

57. What scents do many insects and animals release to court one another?

58. How many minutes does it take for the Hubble Space Telescope to orbit the earth?

59. Because coffee and tea are so popular throughout the world, what substance in these drinks is the world's most popular psychoactive drug?

60. What is a molecule or compound formed by the combination of two identical simple molecules?

# Answers 51-60

51. Absolute Zero

52. Dislocation

53. Brain

54. Polaris (North Star)

55. Impact Event

56. Coralling

57. Pheromones

58. 97

59. Caffeine

60. Dimer

# Questions 61-70

61. Roe, most often sold as caviar, are the eggs of what creatures?

62. Largest of the dwarf planets of our Solar System, this recently-discovered heavenly body was named for the Greek goddess of strife, her Latin name being translated as Discordia.

63. What's the name for the scale used to measure the hotness of a chili pepper based on its amount of heat-producing capsaicin?

64. The opposite angles of this shape have equal measure and the two diagonals are perpendicular. It looks like a kite or diamond and comes from the Greek word for "that spins."

65. What was the name of the U.S.'s first and only space station independently built by the USA?

66. Osteomalacia or rickets is caused by a deficiency of what vitamin?

67. What is the term for muscles and bodily processes like breathing not under conscious control?

68. What medical subspecialty deals with the study and treatment of cancer?

69. Even though resinite can be used as jewelry and can contain fossils, it is not a true mineral, it is fossilized tree sap. What is the common name for this substance.

70. Which element has been known since ancient times and is referred to in the Bible as brimstone? The name may have been derived from the Arabic word "sufra," meaning yellow.

# Answers 61-70

61. Fish

62. Eris

63. Scoville

64. Rhombus

65. Skylab

66. Vitamin D

67. Involuntary

68. Oncology

69. Amber

70. Sulfur

## Questions 71-80

71. Latin for "painter," this constellation was thought to represent a painter's easel.

72. Originally called Apis, or The Bee, this constellation is now given the Latin name for "fly."

73. What belt of space debris exists beyond Neptune and contains three dwarf planets: Haumea, Makemake and Pluto?

74. What breed is often referred to as the "Apollo of Dogs?"

75. The three main bee castes include the queen, the workers and the what?

76. What type of animal was Ham, the astronaut who was contained in Mercury-Redstone 2, in 1961?

77. In the disease AIDS, what does the D stand for?

78. This unfortunately named appetite-suppressant candy was popular in the 1970s and early 1980s until awareness of acquired immunodeficiency syndrome caused sales to drop by nearly 50%.

79. The common distance of the points of a circle from its center is called its what?

80. Roasting wood in a smoldering, smothered fire results in a soft, brittle, lightweight, black, porous material that resembles coal. It's often used to cook your burgers.

# Answers 71-80

71. Pictor

72. Musca

73. Kuiper Belt

74. Great Dane

75. Drones

76. Chimp

77. Deficiency

78. Ayds

79. Radius

80. Charcoal

# Questions 81-90

81. In ancient times, what element was used to produce yellow colored ceramic glazes before it was discovered to be radioactive and better suited for nuclear power plants?

82. What is the loss of bony tissue called that occurs mostly in postmenopausal women that results in fragile bones and loss of height?

83. According to the Beaufort Scale, what wind speed is between 8 and 12 Mph?

84. What prehistoric shark was the inspiration for Peter Benchley's book "Jaws?"

85. Which wronged wife of Othello in Shakespeare's play is also the name of one of Uranus's moons?

86. Seasonal changes are caused when the Earth tilts on its what?

87. What unit of measurement do astronomers use to describe stellar distances?

88. High-energy photons used for medical imaging are called what? People and doctors rely on them when they have broken bones.

89. A negatively charged object has an excess of what subatomic particles?

90. The hardest mineral known on Earth, with a Mohs scale hardness of 10, is what allotrope of carbon?

# Answers 81-90

81. Uranium

82. Osteoporosis

83. Gentle Breeze

84. Megaladon

85. Desdemona

86. Axis

87. Parsecs

88. X-rays

89. Electrons

90. Diamond

# Questions 91-100

91. What effect is a process by which radiative energy (heat) leaving Earth's surface is absorbed by some of the atmospheric gases?

92. Before John Archibald Wheeler named black holes what were they called?

93. This Uranus moon shares the name of characters in several literary works, including "The Tempest, "The Rape of the Lock" and Disney's "The Little Mermaid."

94. When 100% relative humidity is reached, water vapor changes from gas to a liquid through what process?

95. What is the measurement of an amount of substance?

96. Which Space Shuttle was the first fully functioning orbiter?

97. How many languages are included in the Golden Records on the Voyager spacecraft?

98. What electromagnetic wavelengths are also called Roentgen radiation?

99. What medical knife is used to perform surgery?

100. What are the extremely energetic rays called that travel through space at nearly the speed of light and form a great deal of Earth's background radiation? Also the name of a 1962 Bruce Conner film.

# Answers 91-100

91. Greenhouse Effect

92. Frozen Stars

93. Ariel

94. Condensation

95. Mole

96. Columbia

97. 55

98. X-rays

99. Scalpel

100. Cosmic Rays

# Questions 101-110

101. Which rock group are sandstone and shale classified in?

102. Which element is named after the Titans, the sons of the Earth goddess in Greek mythology? It's used in sunscreen since it has strong UV light absorption.

103. What is a whale's penis called?

104. Chloroplasts contain what pigment essential for photosynthesis?

105. What battle-ready dinosaur name means "plated lizard" or "roof lizard"?

106. What wind speed must a storm reach before it is given a name?

107. What is the Great Red Spot on the planet Jupiter?

108. What is the outermost layer of a plant cell?

109. In which layer of Earth's atmosphere do most meteors burn up upon entering the atmosphere, it's name literally means "middle sphere" in Greek?

110. This rock started out as limestone, but once it was exposed to heat and pressure it turned into this rock. Michelangelo's "David" is made of it.

# Answers 101-110

101. Sedimentary

102. Titanium

103. Dork

104. Chlorophyll

105. Stegosaurus

106. 40 Mph

107. A Storm

108. Cell Wall

109. Mesosphere

110. Marble

# Questions 111-120

111. What units do physicists measure work or energy in?

112. This condiment wasn't a tomato-based product until the early 19th century. It was originally a briny mixture that was often made from mushrooms or nuts.

113. The innermost moon of Jupiter is named for this Titan, Zeus's first wife and the mother of Athena and believed to be the embodiment of cunning and wisdom.

114. What geologic era are we in now? Hint: dinosaurs live during the Mesozoic.

115. If air, water and glass are transparent, then concrete, steel and oak represent what antonym of transparent?

116. It may vary from just a few miles to a few hundred miles in width and from the low-tide mark to about 600 feet in depth. Name this submerged border of a continent.

117. What organelle of a cell is used to store food, waste and sometimes water?

118. What form of matter has no surface and will spread out indefinitely?

119. What would you call a sudden, spasmodic contraction of the thoracic cavity?

120. From the Latin word for "garlic," which plant genus contains onions, shallots, leeks, scallions and herbs, such as garlic and chives?

# Answers 111-120

111. Joules

112. Ketchup

113. Metis

114. Cenozoic

115. Opaque

116. Continental Shelf

117. Vacuoles

118. Gas

119. Cough

120. Allium

# Questions 121-130

121. What shape encompasses many others, like the rectangle and rhomboid, because it has 2 pairs of parallel sides and the opposite sides and opposites angles are of equal length and measure?

122. What theory is a developing theory in particle physics that attempts to reconcile quantum mechanics and general relativity? In this theory five dimensions have been named.

123. Secondary ground tremors after a major earthquake that are caused by the repositioning of rock beneath the surface are called what?

124. The phase of the moon as it enlarges from crescent to full is known by what term?

125. Any plastic that can be broken down by bacterial enzymes is described as being what?

126. The emission of alpha and gamma rays from a substance through the decay of the nuclei of its atoms is known as this? Madame Cure was a pioneer in the field.

127. What supercontinent was assembled from large continents like Euramerica, Gondwana and Siberia? It existed from the end of the Permian Period to the Jurassic Period and its name comes from the Greek word for "all lands."

128. At the end of 1859, Charles Darwin's publication of "On the Origin of Species" explained natural selection in detail and presented evidence leading to increasingly wide acceptance of the theory of what?

129. In November 1971, what NASA craft became Mars' first artificial satellite?

130. In science what name is given to a thermal process in which no heat is added or removed from the system?

# Answers 121-130

121. Parallelogram

122. String Theory

123. Aftershocks

124. Waxing

125. Biodegradable

126. Radiation

127. Pangea

128. Evolution

129. Mariner 9

130. Adiabatic Process

## Questions 131-140

131. This Uranus satellite was named for the drunken jester from Shakespeare's "The Tempest."

132. What gas used by dentists is often referred to as laughing gas?

133. Name the columns of calcium carbonate crystals that grow upwards from the floors of caves in carboniferous limestone areas.

134. What is pure water on the pH scale?

135. In the spring and fall there are two days where day and night are of equal length. This refers to what phenomenon?

136. The DPT vaccine protects agains tetanus, pertussis and what other disease?

137. What animal that once numbered in the tens of millions on the prairies of the American west had been reduced to 549 in 1889?

138. This moon of Jupiter is also the name of a nymph favored by Zeus as well as a famous ancient city when pluralized.

139. What is the most common type of iris found in gardens?

140. Which member of the Bonobo community is the leader?

# Answers 131-140

131. Trinculo

132. Nitrous Oxide

133. Stalagmites

134. Neutral

135. Equinox

136. Diptheria

137. Buffalo

138. Thebe

139. Bearded (German) Iris

140. Matriarch

# Questions 141-150

141. Who developed Hyper-Threading technology for their processors?

142. Since a majority of the constellations are representations of his twelve labors, it is only appropriate that one be named for this Greek hero.

143. The abandoned daughter of King Leontes raised by a shepherd in Shakespeare's "The Winter's Tale." She shares her name with a moon of Uranus.

144. What is the name of the chestnut-sized gland at the base of the urethra in men?

145. The snail shaped part of the inner ear is known as what?

146. What is the only moon in our solar system to have its own dense atmosphere?

147. What does it take a female killer whale 15 to 18 months to do, and can only be done once every 5 years?

148. What type of electric power transmission was championed by Thomas Edison?

149. On average, how many "great" earthquakes occur each year? A great earthquake is one that falls between an 8.0-9.9 on the Richter Scale.

150. What "jet propelled" marine creature has a soft, torpedo-shaped body with two flaps used for steering and ten arms with suckers?

# Answers 141-150

141. Intel

142. Hercules

143. Perdita

144. Prostate

145. Cochlea

146. Titan

147. Give Birth

148. Direct Current

149. 1

150. Squid

# Questions 151-160

151. Which mammal communicates through a series of clicks, whistles and other vocalizations?

152. What ocean creature was observed alive for the first time Sept. 30, 2004?

153. Who purchased the Codex Leicester in 1994 for $30.8 million?

154. Where do gastropods carry their foot?

155. What quantum physicist hypothetically placed a cat in a sealed death trap?

156. What word comes from the native Algonquian Indian word meaning "twig eater?"

157. What was the largest of the sabertoothed cats?

158. The hallucinogen mescaline is derived from what cactus?

159. What large planet is named for the the unwilling father of the Titans and Greek god of the sky?

160. Streams that have multiple channels instead of one main channel are called what?

# Answers 151-160

151. Dolphins

152. Giant Squid

153. Bill Gates

154. Stomach

155. Erwin Schrodinger

156. Moose

157. Smilodon

158. Peyote

159. Uranus

160. Braided Streams

# Questions 161-170

161. A nephrolith is a stone formed in what organ?

162. Kinetic energy is energy in motion. What adjective describes energy at rest?

163. Clean the area with an alcohol-soaked cotton ball. Then, using tweezers, grasp it as near to its mouthparts and as close to the skin as you can and steadily pull it up and out, not squeezing or twisting, to remove what?

164. It's produced when the Sun warms one part of the Earth more than another causing warm air to expand and rise to replace cooler, denser air, which then moves along the Earth's surface from other regions.

165. What word is used for volcanic mudflows?

166. What piece of optical equipment is associated with ornithologists?

167. This prolific meteor shower that occurs during late July-early August, sometimes called the Tears of St. Lawrence, derives its name from the constellation it appears to be released from.

168. In physics, identify the property of a body in motion which can be calculated by multiplying it's mass and velocity together.

169. In April 3,1974, an outbreak of what meteorological phenomenon took place across Georgia, Illinois, Indiana, Kentucky, Michigan, Mississippi, North Carolina, Ohio, South Carolina, Tennessee, Virginia and West Virginia?

170. What is the term for the examination and dissection of a body to determine the cause of death?

# Answers 161-170

161. Kidney

162. Potential

163. Tick

164. Wind

165. Lahar

166. Binoculars

167. Perseids

168. Momentum

169. Tornados

170. Autopsy

# Questions 171-180

171. What type of rocks are created from the transformation of pre-existing rock?

172. Allium sativum is a member of the onion family and a commonly used item used to ward off vampires. What's the more common name of this plant?

173. Which type of hardwood tree in the genus Fraxinus has pale wood and shares its name with the residue left after a fire?

174. What "red planet" is named for the Roman god of war?

175. What is a joule?

176. What hardy, large Scottish horse is known for the hairy tufts on its lower legs?

177. What atom is diamond, buckyball, and graphite allotropes of?

178. Which is first alphabetically of the cardinal points on a compass?

179. Originally named to commemorate the victory of King John III Sobieski of Poland, the name of this constellation was shortened to the Latin word for "shield."

180. Whose book "Principia" is generally considered to be one of the most important scientific books ever written?

# Answers 171-180

171. Metamorphic

172. Garlic

173. Ash

174. Mars

175. Unit of Energy

176. Clydesdale

177. Carbon

178. East

179. Scutum

180. Isaac Newton

## Questions 181-190

181. What bitter additive to tonic water is also used to fight the disease malaria?

182. How do mammals classified as Monotremes give birth?

183. How long is an elephant's gestation period?

184. What 5-pointed shape, with points of equal length and angles of 36 degrees at each point, does not have linear edges that join together?

185. Razorbacks are common in the southern U.S. They are the wild ancestors of what domesticated animal?

186. What gland in the neck controls how rapidly the body uses up energy?

187. What term describes the muscular tissue of the human heart?

188. What shape does DNA usually assume?

189. What battle-ready dinosaur name means "plated lizard" or "roof lizard?"

190. Who is the Russian chemist credited with developing the modern periodic table?

## Answers 181-190

181. Quinine

182. Laying Eggs

183. 22 months

184. Star

185. Pig

186. Thyroid

187. Myocardium

188. Double Helix

189. Stegosaurus

190. Mendeleev

# Questions 191-200

191. What Space Shuttle even occurred on July 8, 2011?

192. What compound produces hydrogen ions in a water solution?

193. Pit vipers have two pits under their nostrils that detect what?

194. What Austrian monk is often called the father of genetics?

195. What device on the decks of aircraft carriers functions to accelerate airplanes during takeoff and was also used in medieval times to hurl massive stones at castles?

196. An pneumonectomy is the removal of what organ from the body?

197. The Chumash tribe of California call this constellation "the Lizard" and it is supposed to be one of the ones you encounter before you enter the land of the dead. It's also the Latin word for "lizard."

198. An annulus is what shaped geometric figure formed by the area between two concentric circles?

199. What significant discovery did Jane Goodall make in 1960 while watching chimpanzees?

200. What tall species of bear can reach 13 feet high when standing?

# Answers 191-200

191. Last Flight

192. Acid

193. Heat

194. Gregor Mendel

195. Catapult

196. Lung

197. Lacerta

198. Ring

199. Tool Use

200. Brown Bear

# Questions 201-210

201. In what disease does lung tissue lose its elasticity?

202. This vivid blue semi-precious stone mined in Afghanistan's Badakhshan province and prized by the ancient Egyptians, Mesopotamians, Greeks and Romans has a name that literally means "stone of blue."

203. How many joints are in the human body?

204. On August 4, 1961, Barack Obama was born in this U.S. state.

205. Name the contractile, circular diaphragm forming the colored portion of the eye that shares its name with the Greek goddess of rainbows.

206. The measures of the interior angles of a triangle in Euclidean space always add up to how many degrees?

207. What vertebrate group has the most number of species?

208. On bread, mold produces threads that grow across the surface and periodically shoot upward into little balls. What reproductive structures are inside these balls?

209. What prehistoric relative of the rhinoceros grew to 18 feet tall at the shoulder and had a neck like a giraffe?

210. Cardiac arrhythmia describes what condition in the heart?

# Answers 201-210

201. Emphysema

202. Lapis Lazuli

203. 230

204. Hawaii

205. Iris

206. 180

207. Fish

208. Spores

209. Paraceratherium

210. Irregular Heartbeat

# Questions 211-220

211. What Jurassic-era veggie-saurus had a name meaning "arm lizard?"

212. Where is the bicep muscle located on the human body?

213. A "bible bump" is a colloquial term for what medical condition? It was believed these fluid-filled sacks around the tendons of the hands and wrists could be cured by hitting them with a bible.

214. Which theory is the branch of pure mathematics concerned with the properties of integers, as well as the wider classes of problems that arise from their study?

215. In humans, what arm bone runs from the shoulder down to the elbow?

216. The flat, spreading top of a cumulonimbus could is shaped like what tool associated with blacksmiths?

217. Which species of dolphin is effectively blind due to the large amount of sediment found in its home waters?

218. What is the name given to the scientific study of plant life?

219. The relatively smooth, large circular plains on the moon are called what?

220. The Earth is made up of four main layers. Three of them are (in no specific order) the crust, the inner core and the outer core. What is the fourth layer?

# Answers 211-220

211. Brachiosaurus

212. Upper Arm

213. Ganglion Cyst

214. Number Theory

215. Humerus

216. Anvil

217. Indus River

218. Botany

219. Mariah

220. Mantle

# Questions 221-230

221. In theoretical physics, what theory identifies 11 dimensions? Its creator didn't specify what its name stood for, presumably it could stand for either 'magic', 'mystery', or 'matrix', according to taste.

222. What airtight, metal kitchen device boosts the temperature at which water boils so foods cook faster? It also informally means being in a situation or in an atmosphere of difficulty, stress or anxiety.

223. The amount of product produced during a chemical reaction is known as what?

224. Polytetrafluoroethylene is the chemical name of what popular non-stick coating?

225. Zeus took the form of Artemis and raped this nymph, who was then turned into a bear and killed with a silver bow. The second largest of Jupiter's Galilean moons is named for her.

226. Though famous for putting the snuff on werewolves, silver still packs a wallop on vampires in a few popular literature series. What's the periodic table symbol for silver?

227. What term describes the dried meat of a coconut?

228. This small southern constellation was named for a lizard that can change color to adapt to its environment.

229. What canine-named mineral is an important source of tungsten ore?

230. What is the largest moon to orbit the dwarf planet Pluto?

# Answers 221-230

221. M Theory

222. Pressure Cooker

223. Yield

224. Teflon

225. Callisto

226. Ag

227. Copra

228. Chamaeleon

229. Wolframite

230. Charon

## Questions 231-240

231. What is any quadrilateral with 4 right angles and "oblong," referring to the shape that doesn't have four equal length sides?

232. Who's study of the Kasakela Chimpanzee Community in 1960 led to a greater understanding of their behavior and social structure?

233. What dagger is used in Indo-Malay cultures, often by royalty and sometimes in religious rituals?

234. This pandemic disease was first clinically observed in the U.S. in 1981, and currently infects more than 40 million people worldwide. It played a major role in the pivotal awareness movies "And the Band Played On" and "Philadelphia."

235. What is the name for male gamete cells?

236. James Watson and Francis Crick won Noble Prizes when they discovered the structure of this organic molecule.

237. From the Greek word meaning "love potion," what is the vertical groove on the median line of the upper lip that goes up to the nose?

238. All salamanders live part of their lives in water and part on land. Therefore, they belong to what biological class?

239. Where was the first recorded European contact with chimpanzees in the 17th century?

240. What does the "c" in E=MC^2 stand for?

# Answers 231-240

231. Rectangle

232. Jane Goodall

233. Kris

234. AIDS

235. Spermatozoa

236. DNA

237. Philtrum

238. Amphibians

239. Angola

240. Constant Speed of Light

## Questions 241-250

241. Cyclones and hurricanes occur in which layer of the atmosphere?

242. What is the name shared by the rectangular opening in a film projector in which each frame of film is held stationary while it is exposed and the circular opening through which light enters a camera?

243. What 25-centimeter long muscular tube carries food from the mouth to the stomach?

244. What vitamin is essential in preventing the disease known as scurvy?

245. This famous Arkansan was the founder of the Holiday Inn chain of hotels.

246. A sudden, frenzied charge by a herd of wild animals is called a what?

247. What is the largest living animal with teeth?

248. What elements that make up light act like waves and particles?

249. What type of injury is usually caused by overextending or twisting a limb beyond its normal range of motion?

250. In organisms that reproduce sexually, once a sperm fertilizes an egg cell, the result is a cell called a what?

# Answers 241-250

241. Troposphere

242. Aperture

243. Esophagus

244. Vitamin C

245. Kemmons Wilson

246. Stampede

247. Sperm Whale

248. Photons

249. Sprain

250. Zygote

# Questions 251-260

251. The name of Caliban's mother in Shakespeare's "The Tempest" and one of the alien races in "Doctor Who," it's also one of Uranus' largest irregular satellites.

252. This force is believed to be unimaginably strong in a black hole. It also keeps people from being flung off the Earth.

253. Name the sluggish, tailless, furry arboreal marsupial of Australia that eats only eucalyptus leaves.

254. Approximately how fast is light in a vacuum measured in miles per second (mps)?

255. What term is used when dolphins work together to manipulate small fish into a group for feeding purposes?

256. What is the name of the mechanical barrier that protects London from flooding?

257. The five taste sensations in the tongue are sweet, sour, salty, bitter and what?

258. In what era did the Triassic, Jurassic and Cretaceous periods occur?

259. In medicine, inflammatory cardiomegaly, congestive cardiac failure, hypertensive cardiomyopathy and carditis all have to do with which organ of the human body?

260. This mineral, also called loadstone, can help you find your way home, if you know how to use a compass.

## Answers 251-260

251. Sycorax

252. Gravity

253. Koala

254. 186,000 mps

255. Herding

256. Thames Barrier

257. Savory

258. Mesozoic

259. Heart

260. Magnetite

# Questions 261-270

261. What bird species' wing span averages three meters from tip to tip?

262. What distinctive feature does the Sphynx housecat breed possess?

263. What supercontinent is thought to have formed about 1 billion years ago?

264. What enormous mountain range began to form some 38 million years ago when sediments of the Tethys Sea became crushed and folded as the continental plate bearing India was forced up against the Eurasian plate?

265. Which Mercury astronaut never actually flew any of the Mercury missions?

266. Newton said a force is something applied to a mass that causes it to accelerate either by a push or a what?

267. Have some chaffing? Diaper rash? Stinky feet? Then you probably use this mineral found in powders to remedy your situation.

268. What whale is sometimes referred to as a sea canary because of its high-pitched twitter?

269. In 1999, Mitt Romney took a leave of absence from Bain Capital to organize this event that took place in Salt Lake City in 2002.

270. In chemistry and physics, which theory is a theory of the nature of matter, stating that matter is composed of discrete units made of protons, electrons & neutrons?

# Answers 261-270

261. Great Albatross

262. Virtually Hairless

263. Rodinia

264. Himalayas

265. Deke Slayton

266. Pull

267. Talc

268. Beluga

269. Winter Olympics

270. Atomic Theory

## Questions 271-280

271. What is Otitis Media an infection of?

272. Which Roman goddess of love and beauty lends her name to the second planet from the sun?

273. This Zodiac constellation is named with the Latin term for "goat horn." It's represented by a sea goat, or half goat and half shark.

274. What term describes how much matter an object contains?

275. What is the name for the center section of an insect's body?

276. Which elements are a series of nonmetal elements from of the periodic table, comprising fluorine (F), chlorine (Cl), bromine (Br), iodine (I) & astatine (At)?

277. Which day of the year occurs exactly when the Earth's axial tilt is farthest away from the sun, on December 20 or 22, each year in the Northern Hemisphere?

278. What casino game was created by French mathematician Blaise Pascal while he was doing experiments into a perpetual motion machine?

279. Smallest of the four Galilean moons of Jupiter, what satellite was named for the Phoenician noblewoman who was abducted and raped by Zeus in the form of a white bull and became the first queen of Crete?

280. This ringed planet is named for the Roman god of agriculture, liberation and time.

## Answers 271-280

271. Inner Ear

272. Venus

273. Capricorn

274. Mass

275. Thorax

276. Halogens

277. Winter Solstice

278. Roulette

279. Europa

280. Saturn

## Questions 281-290

281. Which portion of the dolphin's mouth is used to pinpoint the location and size of an object?

282. I'm the element that makes up 65% of your body. By the way, my best friend is hydrogen.

283. Located in the White Mountains of California, which type of tree is the oldest in the U.S. with an age of 4700 years?

284. Name the reflex that involves deep inhalation and exhalation. It's associated with boredom or being tired, and some say it's contagious.

285. What disorder brought on by exposure can be identified by these symptoms: shivering, slurred speech, pale skin and slow breathing?

286. Which of the Apollo missions was the last to include a moonwalk in its mission?

287. What space telescope, to be launched from Ariane 5 in 2014, is the planned successor to the Hubble Space Telescope, named after the second administrator for the NASA Program?

288. What was the largest meating-eating dinosaur?

289. Researchers developed Gatorade in 1965 at what university? Probably why it's got "gator" in the name.

290. Innermost of the four Galilean moons of Jupiter, this volcanically-prolific satellite was named for the priestess of Hera who became Zeus' lover. She was transformed into a heifer and forced to roam the earth being stung by a gadfly.

## Answers 281-290

281. Teeth

282. Oxygen

283. Bristlecone Pine

284. Yawning

285. Hypothermia

286. Apollo 17

287. James Webb

288. Spinosaurus

289. Florida

290. Io

## Questions 291-300

291. According to the Beaufort Scale, at what wind speed will you begin to see whitecaps on the water?

292. In chemistry, what is the term used to describe a solid that separates out from a solution?

293. Contour lines were initially used on a map of the region around the English Channel in 1737. This is the first example of what type of map?

294. After a two and half year effort to rebuild the shuttle program following the fatal Columbia accident, what space shuttle was sent into orbit in July of 2005?

295. Which body system carries nutrients and gases to all parts of the body by way of the blood?

296. Which endocrine gland, situated in the neck, secretes hormones necessary for growth and proper metabolism? It consists of two lobes connected by a narrow segment called the isthmus.

297. When you put your hand on a Van de Graaf generator, your hair stands straight out. What kind of electricity generated by this device causes this?

298. What element does a plant release as a result of photosynthesis?

299. What dinosaur is believed to be the longest that ever lived?

300. What is the name given to water that has atoms of deuterium instead of ordinary hydrogen, useful in nuclear experiments?

## Answers 291-300

291. Gentle Breeze

292. Precipitate

293. Topographic

294. Discovery

295. Circulatory

296. Thyroid

297. Static

298. Oxygen

299. Amphicoelias

300. Heavy

# Questions 301-310

301. How many of the planets in our solar system are named after Greco-Roman myths?

302. What celestial body is nicknamed "The Red Planet?"

303. The physicist J.J. Thomson discovered what tiny charged particles some 1,800 times smaller than the smallest atom? They are responsible for static cling.

304. This Titan, also a moon of Saturn, is credited with being the creator of mankind and is known in popular mythology for stealing fire from Zeus and giving it to humans.

305. What does the passage of an astronomical body through the shadow of another produce?

306. What order of mammals to gerbils, gophers, guinea pigs, hamsters, chinchillas, capybaras, prairie dogs, rats, beavers and squirrels all belong to?

307. What is a path that surrounds an area, from the Greek for "around" and "measure," also known as the length of the outline of a shape?

308. Earthquakes create 2 types of seismic waves. The waves that move faster are called primary waves, the waves that move slower are called what?

309. This astronomical term refers to a stellar explosion that is more energetic than a regular nova and can briefly outshine an entire galaxy.

310. From the Greek for "globe" or "ball," what shape is a perfectly round, geometric object in 3-dimensional space, such as a round ball?

# Answers 301-310

301. 8

302. Mars

303. Electrons

304. Prometheus

305. Eclipse

306. Rodents

307. Perimeter

308. Secondary

309. Supernova

310. Sphere

## Questions 311-320

311. What object in space were all space Shuttle missions required to orbit after the Columbia accident?

312. If you completely avoid any Vitamin C in your diet for the next few months, you could share what disease that afflicted great numbers of 15th-century sailors?

313. What uranium concentrate powder is obtained from leach solutions? It sounds like something you would order in a bakery.

314. Biceps contract when you bend your arm while what other muscle relaxes?

315. What planet has a ring named Gossamer?

316. What is the term for the transfer of characteristics from parent to offspring?

317. What disease is believed to be behind medieval Europe's Black Death?

318. What is the name of the arm of the Milky Way galaxy in which the Earth resides?

319. What unseen substance is theorized to make up 23% of the universe's mass?

320. What name is given to the condition of zero electrical resistivity below the transition temperature of a substance?

# Answers 301-320

311. Space Station

312. Scurvy

313. Yellowcake

314. Triceps

315. Jupiter

316. Heredity

317. Bubonic Plague

318. Orion

319. Dark Matter

320. Superconductivity

## Questions 321-330

321. The three nutrients that the body may use as energy sources include fats, proteins and this, unless you are on the South Beach or Atkins diets.

322. In what kind of triangle are all sides the same length and all angles measure 60 degrees?

323. In the 1670s, a debate began that lasted over 200 years when Isaac Newton said that light consists of tiny particles called corpuscles, while Christian Huygens said it travels instead as these?

324. We all know the four known taste sensations: bitter, salty, sour and sweet. But some scientists now include a fifth taste called what?

325. Your eyes are regularly bathed by tears which wash away any debris that lodges on the clear protective coating of the eye called the what?

326. Neso is the most distant of the known moons of Neptune. It's named after these sea-nymphs who help sailors in peril.

327. What type of classes did Christa McAuliffe plan to teach from her berth inside the space Shuttle Challenger?

328. Second largest of the Uranus moons, it was named for the mythical king of the fairies in Shakespeare's A Midsummer Night's Dream.

329. What kind of skeletons do dragonflies and lobsters have? They're the opposite of internal skeletons.

330. What is the study of animals which are presumed to exist but lack proof?

# Answers 321-330

321. Carbohydrates

322. Equilateral

323. Waves

324. Umami

325. Cornea

326. Nereids

327. Science

328. Oberon

329. Exoskeletons

330. Cryptozoology

## Questions 331-340

331. Small white spots called leukonychia can appear on what human body part?

332. Unless acted on by an external force, a body at rest remains at what?

333. Anatomist Jan Jesenius performed the first what in 1600 in Prague?

334. In what type of symbiotic relationship is one member of the association benefited while the other is harmed? An example: fleas on a dog.

335. According to the Beaufort Scale, what is a wind speed known as when it is between 39-46 MPH?

336. What city in California has a name reminiscent of an exclamation uttered by Archimedes when he discovered the principle of displacement?

337. What term measures the degree of closeness of measurements to its actual (true) value?

338. Wilhelm Rontgen discovered electromagnetic radiation, better known as what, an achievement that earned him the first Nobel Prize in Physics in December 1901?

339. Energy that comes from natural resources such as geothermal heat, rain, sunlight, tides and wind is often called?

340. What did comet Shoemaker-Levy 9 slam into in July, 1994?

# Answers 331-340

331. Nails

332. At Rest

333. Public Human Dissection

334. Parasitic

335. Gale

336. Eureka

337. Accuracy

338. X-Rays

339. Renewable

340. Jupiter

# Questions 341-350

341. What is the Latin name used to describe our sun?

342. Which of the original Mercury astronauts died aboard Apollo 1?

343. Weight is the product of gravity and what?

344. What is the term for solutions that can resist change in pH?

345. This Neptunean moon is named simply for the general term for the sea-nymphs and attendants of the god Poseidon.

346. The largest of Saturn's moons is named for the elder gods who were overthrown by the Olympians in Greek mythology.

347. The inability to tolerate gluten in foods is known as what?

348. What type of dwarf star produces the least amount of heat?

349. Hardwoods come from deciduous trees. Softwoods, including pinecones, come from what other kind of trees?

350. DNA contains the genetic instructions used in the development and functioning of all known living organisms. What does the "N" stand for in DNA?

# Answers 341-350

341. Sol

342. Gus Grissom

343. Mass

344. Buffers

345. Nereid

346. Titan

347. Celiac disease

348. Red Dwarf

349. Conifers

350. Nucleic

# Questions 351-360

351. At the cannery, machines cut off the ends and remove the cores before what fruit is cut into chunks or crushed?

352. What is the allotrope of oxygen that contains 3 atoms in one molecule?

353. Which metal has evidence suggesting it was being separated from lead as early as 3000 B.C.?

354. What useful Scrabble 2-letter word refers to volcanic lava?

355. What is the name for a young eel?

356. Besides echidnas, this is the only other mammal that doesn't have an umbilical scar, or belly button? Name this aquatic Australian mammal.

357. What is the softest mineral on the Mohs scale of hardness?

358. What is the hardest mineral on the Mohs scale of hardness?

359. Pharyngitis, tonsillitis and laryngitis all affect which part of the body?

360. What type of whale, caught near Alaska in 2007, had an explosive harpoon embedded in its blubber that was believed to be from a whale hunt over 100 years prior?

# Answers 351-360

351. Pineapples

352. Ozone

353. Silver

354. AA

355. Elver

356. Platypus

357. Talc

358. Diamond

359. Throat

360. Bowhead Whale

## Questions 361-370

361. This moon of Uranus was named for the daughter of the banished Duke in Shakespeare's "As You Like It."

362. Which line delineates space from outer space?

363. Just like a mollusk's shell, in which it is found, this is made up of calcium carbonate in minute crystalline form that has been deposited in concentric layers.

364. What must happen to planets in order for there to be an "impact event?"

365. What do gelotologists study?

366. I am a bright yellow element in my natural form and I contribute to the rotten egg smell.

367. Chief mother of all the rivers of the world and the name of a prehistoric ocean, this Titan sea goddess lends her name to one of the moons of Saturn.

368. What Jupiter moon is suspected to contain salt water under its frozen surface?

369. When an impact breaks some internal water-containing structures of a fruit, the resulting soft spot is called a what? In humans it's called a contusion or minor hematoma.

370. This stone is great for pedicures and it's the only rock that floats in water. Name this porous stone.

## Answers 361-370

361. Rosalind

362. Karman

363. Pearls

364. Celestial Collision

365. Laughter

366. Sulfur

367. Tethys

368. Europa

369. Bruise

370. Pumice

# Questions 371-380

371. What dwarf planet in our solar system was named for the Roman goddess of agriculture, motherly relationships and fertility?

372. Along with carbon and oxygen, I am the other main element that makes up the shells of clams and oysters.

373. In oceans, what is there plenty of in the photic zone, full of algae and plant life, yet not enough of in the aphotic zone?

374. Which planet's collision with Shoemaker Levy-9 was the first observed major impact event?

375. What is the number of cycles per unit of time called?

376. Which moon of Jupiter is named for the she-goat believed to have suckled infant-god Zeus when he was hidden by his mother from Cronus?

377. What Jurassic-era veggie-saurus had a name meaning "arm lizard"?

378. What human organ secretes hydrochloric acid?

379. The apparent intersection of the Earth and sky as seen by an observer is known as what?

380. What substance does the large intestine reclaim for the body?

# Answers 371-380

371. Ceres

372. Calcium

373. Sunlight

374. Jupiter

375. Frequency

376. Amalthea

377. Brachiosaurus

378. Stomach

379. Horizon

380. Water

# Questions 381-390

381. In chemistry what term is used to name the concentration of a solution expressed in moles of solute per kilogram of solvent?

382. Where would you find the scapula bones on the human body?

383. What's the top number of a fraction called?

384. What celestial objects were thought to be catastrophic omens in ancient times?

385. What two citizenships did Einstein possess when he died?

386. What dinosaur did paleontologist Othniel Marsh name after the discovery of its fossil near Denver, Colorado in 1889?

387. Hyperventilation reduces the quantity of what gas in the blood? It is also the same gas taken in by plants to make oxygen.

388. Largest of the non-Galilean moons of Jupiter, what satellite was named for the nymph enamored of Zeus who bore him three sons.

389. What dinosaur did paleontologist Othniel Marsh name after the discovery of its fossil near Denver, Colorado, in 1889?

390. The defect of the eye known as myopia is also called what?

# Answers 381-390

381. Molality

382. Shoulder Blades

383. Numerator

384. Comets

385. American & Swiss

386. Triceratops

387. Carbon Dioxide

388. Himalia

389. Triceratops

390. Near-sightedness

# Questions 391-400

391. What typically black-handled and double-edged ritual knife is used in Wicca and other derivative forms of Neopagan witchcraft?

392. The Soviet launching of the Sputnik satellites in 1957 prompted Eisenhower to create what agency, responsible for putting the first man on the moon?

393. What branch of internal medicine is concerned specifically with blood?

394. What do the ankle spurs of the male platypus contain?

395. What spotted predator hunts a wider variety of prey than other African big cats?

396. What kind of light used in welding, surgery and CD players can also destroy incoming missiles, or so we'd like to believe?

397. What is the more common name for the Einstein-Rosen Bridge?

398. What type of clay takes its name from the Italian word meaning "baked earth?"

399. What flying toy is a quadrilateral with two pairs of adjacent congruent sides and the measure of the angle formed by the intersection of any two sides is less than 180 degrees?

400. What gland regulates the rate of metabolism in humans?

# Answers 391-400

391. Athame

392. NASA

393. Hematology

394. Venom

395. Leopard

396. Laser

397. Wormhole

398. Terracotta

399. Kite

400. Thyroid

# Questions 401-410

401. What is the second most common type of cancer in men in the U.S.?

402. What biome covers only six percent of the Earth's surface but contains half of the world's species?

403. What is the name of the oldest known research chimp, born in a laboratory on May 21, 1954, in the United States?

404. Newton's first law is often referred to as the Law of what, stating that an object has the tendency to remain at rest or to remain in motion?

405. Wife of Tyndareus and mother of Helen of Troy, Clytemnestra, Castor and Pollux, which mythological figure was seduced by Zeus in the guise of a swan and thus has a moon of Jupiter named for her?

406. Who is regarded as the founder of quantum theory?

407. What type of disease did Bruce Rothschild discover in the fossilized finger bones of the T. Rex named Sue that was discovered in Hell Creek , South Dakota?

408. What was the only planet, at the time, in the solar system discovered in the 1900s?

409. Peggy Lee turned this song into a popular hit in 1960, but most people recognize it as the name for the symptom involving a body temperature above 100 degrees F?

410. A physician who specializes in diseases of the structure, function, and diseases of the nervous system is known as what?

## Answers 401-410

401. Prostate

402. Rain Forest

403. Wenka

404. Inertia

405. Leda

406. Max Planck

407. Gout

408. Pluto

409. Fever

410. Neurologist

# Questions 411-420

411. The atmosphere protects life on Earth by absorbing what kind of solar radiation from the sun?

412. What is the shape produced when a circle has a segment of another circle removed from its edge, so that what remains is a shape enclosed by two arcs of different diameters which intersect at two points?

413. The first artificial heart is known by what name?

414. What do you call compounds that form hydroxyl ions when dissolved in water? It's the opposite of an acid.

415. Jonas Salk was an American medical researcher and virologist, best known for his discovery and development of the first safe and effective vaccine against what disease?

416. What is the clinical term for the soft, waxy, yellow-brown material secreted by the sebaceous glands of the external ear?

417. Ptolemy named this constellation after the famed winged horse of Greek mythology.

418. Potassium nitrate, also known as saltpeter, charcoal and sulfur are the traditional ingredients of what explosive substance?

419. What human organ aids in the destruction of old red blood cells?

420. Quartz, one of the crust's most common minerals, has what crystalline shape?

## Answers 411-420

411. Ultraviolet

412. Crescent

413. Jarvik heart

414. Base

415. Polio

416. Cerumen

417. Pegasus

418. Gunpowder

419. Spleen

420. Hexagonal

# Questions 421-430

421. Which Zodiac constellation is represented as a ram?

422. Small and faint, which constellation shares its name with the Latin word for a mariner's compass?

423. What are the most powerful explosions in the universe called?

424. What do you call the common operation through which one's tonsils are removed?

425. In 1910, thousands and perhaps millions were convinced that the end of the world was at hand. The cause of this prognosis was the anticipated passage of what heavenly body that had not been seen for 76 years?

426. What radiation forms the highest energy end of the electromagnetic spectrum?

427. An octopus has three of these organs. Name this chief organ of the circulatory system.

428. Which state is home to the Badlands Observatory?

429. What is the joining of two small nuclei to form a large nucleus called?

430. What unit do we use to measure electrical power?

## Answers 421-430

421. Aries

422. Pyxis

423. Gamma Ray Bursts

424. Tonsillectomy

425. Halley's Comet

426. Gamma Rays

427. Hearts

428. South Dakota

429. Fusion

430. Watt

# Questions 431-440

431. Which Pluto moon, its largest, is named for the ferryman of the dead in Greek mythology.

432. What organelles in animals contain their own DNA outside a cell's nucleus?

433. What major human organ contains the areas that produce insulin for the body?

434. What type of rock is ejected from volcanoes and so light weight that it floats in water. Hint: you may use it on your feet.

435. What is the main artery of the thigh?

436. Hypokalemia is caused by a deficiency of what element in the body?

437. What rock that can be split into thin sheets and is often used for billiard tables?

438. Whose theorem states the sum of the squares of the lengths of the two legs is equal to the square of the length of the hypotenuse?

439. What astronomer is considered by most to be the father of planetary science and, in addition, has a belt name after him?

440. What did Yuji Hyakutake discover has a tail measuring 354 million miles long?

## Answers 431-440

431. Charon

432. Mitochondria

433. Pancreas

434. Pumice

435. Femoral

436. Potassium

437. Slate

438. Pythagoras

439. Kuiper

440. Comet

# Questions 441-450

441. What substance that determines the shape of ears and noses also composes the skeletons of sharks and rays?

442. John Scopes was brought to trial in Tennessee in 1925 for teaching about what?

443. What layer of human skin contains no blood vessels?

444. What fundamental force of nature causes us to have weight?

445. A test to record the electrical activity in the brain is known as what?

446. In what year was the Voyager 1 deep space probe launched?

447. The study of human history and prehistory through the excavation of sites and the analysis of physical remains is known as what?

448. What bone is the bottom segment in the human spine?

449. Used extensively in musical instruments such as horns and bells for its acoustic properties, brass is a combination of copper what other metal?

450. Amounting to less than one thousandth of the Earth's total volume, it's the outermost layer of the planet.

# Answers 441-450

441. Cartilage

442. Evolution

443. Epidermis

444. Gravity

445. EEG

446. 1977

447. Archaeology

448. Coccyx

449. Zinc

450. Crust

# Questions 451-460

451. The larva of a moth or butterfly is called a what? It's also a brand of heavy machinery.

452. Cheetahs can purr while they inhale, but they cannot do what?

453. The parts of plant foods that your body can't digest or absorb are called roughage, bulk or dietary what?

454. What is the distinctive color of the mineral azurite?

455. What amorphous mineraloid is a birthstone for the month of October?

456. What part of the small intestine connects to the stomach?

457. What are Jupiter's moons' Ganymede, Callisto, Europa, and Io collectively known as?

458. The innermost of Saturn's moons was named for this randy Greek god of shepherds, mountain wilds, flocks and rustic music. He's usually portrayed as having the hindquarters and horns of a goat.

459. Known as the Hunter, which constellation contains the stars Betelgeuse and Rigel?

460. The change of plant and animal forms over vast periods of time is called what, supposedly discovered by Charles Darwin.

# Answers 451-460

451. Caterpillar

452. Roar

453. Fiber

454. Blue

455. Opal

456. Duodenum

457. Galilean Moons

458. Pan

459. Orion

460. Evolution

# Questions 461-470

461. What do mountain climbers and skiers call the temporary loss of vision caused by the sunburning of the cornea?

462. The brightest star in this Zodiac constellation is Spica. It was named for the Latin word meaning "virgin."

463. Algae will produce hydrogen instead of oxygen when deprived of what element?

464. One joule of work per coulomb--the unit of electrical potential transferred--is known as a what?

465. Despite the implication of its name, most have 15-23 segments rather than 100. Name these arthropods.

466. What was the name of the first space Shuttle to fly into orbit?

467. How long does it take the International Space Station to orbit the Earth?

468. Who was the first person to dive solo into Challenger Deep - the deepest point in the Mariana Trench?

469. What type of rock is pumice classified as?

470. What dinosaur became the third largest carnivorous dinosaur after Giganosaurus and Carcharondontosaurus were discovered?

# Answers 461-470

461. Snow Blindness

462. Virgo

463. Sulfur

464. Volt

465. Centipedes

466. Columbia

467. 92 minutes

468. James Cameron

469. Igneous

470. Tyrannosaurus Rex

# Questions 471-480

471. What abbreviated term for a quasi-stellar radio source refers to a very energetic and distant galaxy with an active galactic nuclease. It is also the most luminous object in the universe.

472. The scientific name for fool's gold is?

473. What man's invention of the safety pin made diapers much more convenient to use?

474. What classification is Earth in the fictional classification systems for planets in the "Star Trek" science fiction franchise?

475. What do we call the chain of chemical building blocks in strands of DNA?

476. What type of snake gained more than 75,000 followers on Twitter within 24 hours when it escaped from New York's Bronx Zoo in 2011?

477. This famous Arkansan was an architect and the only apprentice of Frank Lloyd Wright to have received the AIA Gold Medal.

478. Name the four Jovian planets.

479. What type of electromagnetic radiation causes sunburns?

480. Smaller of the two moons of Mars, this satellite was named for one of the sons of Ares and Aphrodite and the personification of terror.

# Answers 471-480

471. Quasar

472. Pyrite

473. Thomas Hunt

474. Class M

475. Nucleotides

476. Egyptian Cobra

477. Fay Jones

478. Jupiter, Saturn, Uranus, Neptune

479. Ultraviolet

480. Deimos

## Questions 481-490

481. In the early 1930s, a psychologist at what southern University tested for ESP using Zener Cards to see if subjects could guess a card without being able to see it?

482. Another name for Semele, the mother of Dionysus by Zeus, this was one of the love conquests of Zeus fated to become a moon of Jupiter.

483. You're driving along a highway at a good clip when you hit a long puddle on the road and suddenly find yourself unable to steer the car. Name this scary phenomenon.

484. What is the scientific term for one billionth of a second?

485. What metric unit is equivalent to 1/1000 of a gram?

486. What subatomic particle is identical in mass to a proton, neutron, or electron, but with the opposite charge?

487. What locker room ailment is most often called "jock itch"?

488. What space shuttle name did "Star Trek" fans desire when they lobbied for changing the name of the Constitution?

489. What is the most abundant element on Earth, making up more than 46.6% of its mass?

490. What element has an atomic number of 3?

# Answers 481-490

481. Duke

482. Lysithea

483. Hydroplaning

484. Nanosecond

485. Milligram

486. Antimatter

487. Tinea Cruris

488. Enterprise

489. Oxygen

490. Lithium

# Questions 491-500

491. What is Thomas A. Swift's electric rifle better known as?

492. What is any substance containing free ions that make the substance electrically conductive? The most typical is an ionic solution.

493. In botany, what type of plant doesn't loose its leaves in the winter, contrasting with deciduous plants, which completely lose their foliage during winter?

494. In 1654, Robert Bissaker invented what tool used for making precise calculations? This tool was widely used into the mid 20th century.

495. What is the largest naturally occurring atom?

496. If a person's blood fails to clot, they suffer from what disorder?

497. Sonar works like radar in locating objects, except instead of radio signals, sonar uses what kind of waves?

498. What type of rock is formed when magma cools and solidifies?

499. What is the common collective name for large, more or less spherical, multi-colored plants that break away from their roots in autumn and scatter their seeds as the wind causes them to roll about?

500. What animal has the largest brain of any animal?

# Answers 491-500

491. A Taser

492. Electrolyte

493. Evergreen

494. Slide Rule

495. Uranium

496. Hemophilia

497. Sound

498. Igneous

499. Tumbleweeds

500. Sperm Whale

# Questions 501-510

501. In medicine, what is the general term referring to a sterile solution of sodium chloride (NaCl) in water?

502. An anemometer measuring wind speed is usually paired with what other device indicating wind direction?

503. What traditional Finnish or Scandinavian style woodcraft belt-knife is used as a tool rather than a weapon?

504. Named for the beautiful daughter of Duke Prospero in Shakespeare's "The Tempest," this is also the name of one of Uranus' moons.

505. What is the length of a line segment whose endpoints lie on the circle and passes through the center of the circle? It's the largest distance between any two points on the circle.

506. What is the name for the crossbreed hybrid of a male tiger and a female lion?

507. Along what rock fractures do most earthquakes take place?

508. What type of insect was introduced in Australia to kill Prickly Pears?

509. What is the common name for the two species of ape in the Pan genus?

510. What is the condition in which the rate of a forward process is exactly the same as the rate of a reverse process?

# Answers 501-510

501. Saline

502. Wind Vane

503. Puukko

504. Miranda

505. Diameter

506. Tigon

507. Faults

508. Moth

509. Chimpanzee

510. Dynamic Equilibrium

## Questions 511-520

511. What element reacts with water to form hypochlorous acid and hypochlorites?

512. He devoted his life to the teaching of deaf-mutes and invented machines such as the graphophone and photophone. Who is this man best known for inventing the telephone in 1876?

513. What man invented a machine for spinning cotton, which he called a spinning frame, in 1768?

514. What cell results from the merging of an ovum with a sperm?

515. What is the theory of the structure of spacetime, first introduced by Albert Einstein in his 1905 paper, "On the Electrodynamics of Moving Bodies?"

516. This describes what kind of hazard: Moving at speeds approaching 200 miles per hour, these can scour 3000 feet of mountainside in 15 seconds with impact pressures of more than 20,000 pounds per square foot.

517. What is the name of the Hurricane Scale that categorizes hurricanes by the intensity of their winds?

518. What Australian bird is known for its call, which echoes human laughter?

519. It's the second tallest memorial in the United States, located La Porte, TX, and memorializing those who contributed to the independence of Texas.

520. What constellation is named for the Latin word meaning a net of crosshairs on a telescope eyepiece used to measure star positions? It's a small constellation in the southern sky.

# Answers 511-520

511. Chlorine

512. Alexander Graham Bell

513. Richard Arkwright

514. Zygote

515. Theory of Relativity

516. Avalanches

517. Saffir-Simpson

518. Kookaburra

519. San Jacinto Monument

520. Reticulum

# Questions 521-530

521. What color is the longest wavelength of light?

522. A polygon with 6 edges and 6 vertices, the total of the internal angles is 720 degrees, is what shape? A beehive honeycomb is this shape.

523. Which faint constellation is named for the type of artist who would carve his works from marble?

524. The site directly above, below, or at the point of greatest destruction of a nuclear weapon or other catastrophic event is called ground what?

525. Which member of the dolphin family is the largest?

526. What line segment passes through the center of a circle and has its endpoints on the circle?

527. What wind speed must a storm reach in order to be classified as a hurricane?

528. What is the isotope of hydrogen that has one neutron called?

529. In the battle between the Gigantes and the Olympian gods, this Greek figure was disabled by a spear thrown by Athena and was eventually buried on Mount Etna. The volcanic fires of Etna are said to be his breath.

530. Formally known as lachrymator, what is the common name for the chemical compound that stimulates the corneal nerves in the eyes, causing tearing, pain and even blindness?

## Answers 521-530

521. Red

522. Hexagon

523. Sculptor

524. Zero

525. Orca

526. Diameter

527. 74 Mph

528. Deuterium

529. Enceladus

530. Tear Gas

# Questions 531-540

531. The Sun's corona is most visible during what astronomical event?

532. Which vitamin aids the body's use of calcium and phosphorus for healthy bones and teeth and can be made by the body when exposed to sunlight?

533. There are hundreds of common household uses for Arm and Hammer Baking Soda, from cleaning teeth to killing odors. What's the chemical compound for baking soda?

534. There are approximately 950,000 types of what invertebrates?

535. What is infectious mononucleosis also known as in North America?

536. Icebergs float because what property of ice is lower than that of water?

537. Three tomatoes are walking down the street, a poppa tomato, a momma tomato, and a little baby tomato. Baby tomato starts lagging behind. Poppa tomato gets angry, goes over to the baby tomato, squishes him and says..."

538. What does a lapidist specialize in working with?

539. Degraded to a dwarf planet, it shares its name with both the Roman god of the Underworld and Mickey Mouse's pet dog.

540. What organelle is referred to as the post office of a cell?

## Answers 531-540

531. Solar Eclipse

532. Vitamin D

533. Sodium Bicarbonate

534. Insects

535. Kissing Disease

536. Density

537. Ketchup

538. Stones

539. Pluto

540. The Golgi apparatus

## Questions 541-550

541. In chemistry, "cohesion" is the term for the attraction of like molecules. What is the term for the force of attraction between unlike molecules?

542. What degree of burn is a mild sunburn?

543. What type of simple machine consists of a rope and a wheel?

544. James Black created what fixed-blade fighting knife first popularized in the early 19th century at a duel known as the Sandbar Fight?

545. This American astronaut has been into space three times, notably as commander of Apollo 17 in 1972, the final Apollo lunar landing. He's one of the few to have stood on the Moon.

546. What name is given to the glowing electrical charge at the top of tall pointed objects during stormy weather?

547. In 1898, what element did William Ramsay and Morris Travers discover during experiments with liquid air? The name comes from the Greek word meaning "new."

548. What's the central region of a star, planet or galaxy is called? It's also the center of an apple.

549. These are all members of what biological class: caimans, mambas, geckos, terrapins and asps?

550. The largest moon in the solar system and largest of the Galilean moons, it is named for this most-beautiful young lad, kidnapped by an eagle by Zeus and brought to Mount Olympus to serve as the cup-bearer to the gods.

# Answers 541-550

541. Adhesion

542. First Degree

543. Pulley

544. Bowie

545. Eugene Cernan

546. St. Elmo's Fire

547. Neon

548. Core

549. Reptiles

550. Ganymede

# Questions 551-560

551. The Hawaiian volcano Kilauea has been continuously erupting since what year?

552. What is the energy that an object has as a result of motion?

553. Depending on your age, you might have used this rock every day in grade school. It's comprised of coccolithophorids, or fossilized single-cell algae.

554. What bloodsucker uses its funnel-like mouth to bore into other fish?

555. Largest of the moons of Uranus, this satellite shares a name with the queen of the faeries in Shakespeare's "A Midsummer Night's Dream."

556. Which element (symbol At) is the most rare element on earth? It comes from the Greek word meaning "unstable," and is highly radioactive.

557. What animal supposedly causes more human deaths than any other African mammal?

558. A Cretan spirit associated with Demeter, which mythological figure was the mother of Britomartis by Zeus and the name of one of the moons of Jupiter?

559. Because of its erratic orbit, what is sometimes the eighth planet from the sun?

560. What speedy shark can leap up to 20 feet in the air from the water?

# Answers 551-560

551. 1983

552. Kinetic Energy

553. Chalk

554. Lamprey

555. Titania

556. Astatine

557. Hippopotamus

558. Carme

559. Pluto

560. Shortfin Mako Shark

# Questions 561-560

561. What is a measure of the number of chemical bonds formed by the atoms of a given element?

562. In medicine, what word describes a severe and rapid allergic reaction?

563. Who became the first human to travel into space in 1961?

564. In 1990, what country became the third to have a spacecraft orbit the moon?

565. What was the last name of the husband and wife scientist team of Pierre and Marie?

566. Sometimes when a rock is cracked open a fossil appears as a thin black film. This film consists of what element?

567. Named after an Italian mathematician, name the sequence of numbers in which each number is the sum of the previous two numbers?

568. What type of shark is second only to the Great White in human fatalities?

569. What is the closest extant relative of the Orca?

570. Which element's Latin name is ferrum?

# Answers 561-570

561. Valence

562. Anaphylaxis

563. Yuri Gagarin

564. Japan

565. Curie

566. Carbon

567. Fibonacci

568. Tiger

569. Snubfin Dolphin

570. Iron

# Questions 571-580

571. Which metal is found in high concentrations in the meat of dolphins, making them inedible for humans?

572. What is the only other member of the Monodontidae family of cetaceans besides the Beluga Whale?

573. What color of milk do mama hippo's produce?

574. What moon of Neptune is named for the sea nymph daughter born when Poseidon took the form of a stallion and ravished Demeter in the form of a mare?

575. What type of bonds hold atoms together by the sharing of electrons?

576. What type of triangle has all sides of unequal length and the three angles are also all different measures?

577. What international standard units do scientists use to measure pressure?

578. Which tragic love interest of Hamlet, who goes mad at her father's death and drowns herself in the Shakespeare play, gives her name to one of Uranus' moons?

579. What is the name for the process in which a very heavy nucleus splits to from 2 medium weight nuclei?

580. The three units used to measure longitude and latitude are degrees, minutes and what?

# Answers 571-580

571. Mercury

572. Narwhal

573. Pink

574. Despina

575. Covalent Bond

576. Scalene

577. Pascals

578. Ophelia

579. Fission

580. Seconds

# Questions 581-590

581. Which age sits between the Stone and Bronze Ages? Named for metal used extensively during that time, it derived its name from the Latin word "cuprum," meaning "metal of Cyprus."

582. The path followed by a hurricane is called a storm what?

583. What law states the amount of gas dissolved in a solution is directly proportional to the pressure of the gas above the solution?

584. What is a disease that spreads quickly throughout the human population called?

585. Lemon-lime and orange were the only two Gatorade flavors for nearly 20 years until the addition of what new flavor in 1983?

586. What is the name of the round organ located in the head of a dolphin that is used in echolocation?

587. Which human disease occurs naturally in dolphins?

588. Plantlike organisms, such as mushrooms and bread molds, belong to what taxonomic kingdom?

589. What use have Indo-Pacific bottlenose dolphins found for sponges?

590. In 1957, what Russian dog was the first mammal to orbit the Earth?

# Answers 581-590

581. Copper

582. Track

583. Henry's Law

584. Epidemic

585. Fruit Punch

586. Melon

587. Type 2 Diabetes

588. Fungus

589. Nose Protection

590. Laika

# Questions 591-600

591. Largest of the southern sky constellations, this name is derived from the mythological half-man, half-horse creature.

592. What is the element responsible for the vivid blue color seen in glass making, glazes & ceramics?

593. Which space shuttle deployed the Hubble Space Telescope into space?

594. If you take a deep breath and jump into a pond, you will have difficulty remaining submerged because what force keeps pushing you up?

595. What marine mammal is known for its distinctive "unicorn-like" horn?

596. Guglielmo Marconi is famous for what method of detecting the position and velocity of distant objects from radio waves reflected from their surfaces?

597. What mineral is common in the copper deposits around Lake Superior?

598. How many of the Apollo space missions were manned flights?

599. What does a dolphin do with its blowhole?

600. Which constellation of the Zodiac represents two fishes?

## Answers 591-600

590. Laika

591. Centaurus

592. Cobalt

593. Discovery

594. Buoyancy

595. Narwhal

596. Radar

597. Datolite

598. 11

599. Breathe

600. Pisces

# Questions 601-610

601. A material object from a specific culture, such as a tool, an article of clothing, or a prepared food is known as a what?

602. What freshwater fish is famed for its prominent whiskers, or barbels?

603. What marine mammal is known to eat gray whales and great white sharks?

604. Which constellation gets its name from the Greek word for "unicorn?"

605. The mathematicians of Babylon devised a system of counting based on the number 60, from which we get the number of degrees in a circle and the number of minutes in a what?

606. Which monster in Shakespeare's "The Tempest" is also one of Uranus' moons?

607. What is the largest surviving marsupial in the world?

608. What early hominid had a brain roughly one-third the size of homosapiens?

609. What do we call electromagnetic radiation that is visible to the eye?

610. According to the Beaufort Scale, what is a wind speed known as when it is between 39 and 46 Mph?

# Answers 601-610

601. Artifact

602. Catfish

603. Killer Whale

604. Monoceros

605. Hour

606. Caliban

607. Red Kangaroo

608. Australopithecus

609. Light

610. Gale

# Questions 611-620

611. What percentage of the world's earthquakes occur in the Pacific ring of fire?

612. What element are newer pennies mostly comprised of?

613. What neurological disorder is characterized by recurrent episodes of convulsive seizures?

614. In plain English it's the ratio of any circle's circumference to its diameter, and as a Greek letter it's known as what?

615. What Belgian-born US chemist invented the first commercial plastic made from formaldehyde and phenol? The plastic was named for him.

616. What is the sixth planet from the sun?

617. What British scientist was the first to demonstrate how blood circulated through the body?

618. What eating disorder follows overeating with episodes of self-induced vomiting?

619. What are liquid rocks underground called?

620. The groove located in the middle portion of the upper lip, just below the nose, is known as what?

# Answers 611-620

611. 0.9

612. Zinc

613. Epilepsy

614. Psi

615. Baekland

616. Saturn

617. William Harvey

618. Bulimia

619. Magma

620. Philtrum

# Questions 621-627

621. What is the longest venomous snake in the Western Hemisphere?

622. What prominent and prehensile appendage typical of monkeys is entirely lacking on apes, and also on humans?

623. Heat from a fire is transferred by what method of energy transfer?

624. What planet was named after the Roman god of war?

625. The study of the effects of changing temperature, volume, or pressure on a macroscopic scale is known as what?

626. The atomic orbital is the region where what part of the atom can be found?

627. What disease causes the tissue of the liver shrink and harden, and is associated with the consumption of alcohol?

# Answers 621-627

621. Bushmaster

622. Tails

623. Radiation

624. Mars

625. Thermodynamics

626. Electron

627. Cirrhosis

# ABOUT THE AUTHOR

Dr. Seven Phoenix (Doc) has hosted several popular pub trivia nights in Eugene, Oregon since early 2008. Seven Phoenix grew up in Pennsylvania, before moving to the Pacific Northwest, where he earned his Ph.D. in Sociology. Doc loves spending time with his English Mastiff, Kinsey, and enjoys hiking and exploring the Pacific Northwest (in the three months of the year when it isn't raining). You can email Doc at: Se7enPhoenix@gmail.com or follow him on twitter @Se7enPhoenix.

www.ingramcontent.com/pod-product-compliance
Lightning Source LLC
Chambersburg PA
CBHW071406280526
45787CB00001B/459